Risk in Challenging Behaviour

a good practice guide for professionals

Sharon Powell

British Library Cataloguing in Publication Data

A CIP record for this book is available from the Public Library

© BILD Publications 2005

BILD Publications is the imprint of:
British Institute of Learning Disabilities
Campion House
Green Street
Kidderminster
Worcestershire DY10 1JL

Telephone: 01562 723010
Fax: 01562 723029
E-mail: enquiries@bild.org.uk
Website: www.bild.org.uk

ISBN 1 904082 95 5

BILD Publications are distributed by:
BookSource
32 Finlas Street
Cowlairs Estate
Glasgow G22 5DU

Telephone: 08702 402 182
Fax: 0141 557 0189

For a publications catalogue with details of all BILD books and journals telephone 01562 723010, e-mail enquiries@bild.org.uk or visit the BILD website www.bild.org.uk

The British Institute of Learning Disabilities is committed to improving the quality of life for people with a learning disability by involving them and their families in all aspects of our work, working with government and public bodies to achieve full citizenship, undertaking beneficial research and development projects and helping service providers to develop and share good practice.

Contents

Foreword

Twenty years ago the policy of deinstitutionalisation was gathering momentum amid tremendous optimism about the potential that life in the community could offer service users of the future. Greater presence in the community would lead inevitably to a network of more and better relationships. There would be increased scope for people with disabilities to learn and do things appropriate to their age and ability. People would have more control over life-defining matters, such as where and with whom they would live, as well as small everyday decisions, such as what to eat and how to use their time. The cumulative impact of these accomplishments would leave people feeling better about themselves and how others viewed them.

Discussions about risk in those days centred mainly on extending the right to people with intellectual and developmental disabilities to make mistakes and learn from the consequences of those mistakes in the same way as their non-disabled counterparts. Risk was conceptualised as an integral part of life – a dignifying and highly valued aspect of everyday living that was to be embraced in the pursuit of an ordinary life for people whose support needs were far from ordinary.

Twenty years on and the pattern of residential services for people with intellectual impairment has indeed changed. People with intellectual and developmental disabilities, including many whose behaviour is experienced as challenging, now live mainly in small community homes alongside persons with no apparent disabilities. Service providers aspire to facilitate community integration, personal autonomy, development and growth, rights and choice. But the societal context within which these outcomes are pursued has also changed. Nowhere is this more evident than in the way services are expected to think about and manage the personal and organisational risks associated with supporting ordinary life experiences among people whose support needs are complex and challenging.

As a society we are arguably less tolerant of mistakes, and individuals expect to be compensated when things go wrong. We have legislated extensively to protect people from exploitation and harm in many areas of life. Inspectorates, codes of practice and professional codes of conduct tightly regulate both public and private sector activity. As a consequence modern service organisations are highly sensitised to the risks they face in the form of litigation, financial compensation and inflated insurance premiums. Increased public accountability has undoubtedly helped to drive up both expectations and performance standards. But, if aspirations of community living for people with complex and challenging needs are to be realised, we must be careful to avoid stifling innovation and inadvertently robbing individuals of the dignity of risk. In short, we must ensure risks are effectively identified and managed – not simply avoided.

Supporting people with intellectual and developmental disabilities so they can prosper and grow in community settings in spite of challenging behaviours is a complex and difficult task requiring carefully crafted management and delivery. No longer are we satisfied with mere containment and public protection. Services and staff must simultaneously promote for each service user active engagement, social participation, autonomy, development and growth. They must also provide effective treatment interventions to ameliorate the negative effects of challenging behaviours, maintain and defend individual rights and responsibilities and protect people from potential harm. At the same time service organisations have a duty to protect their staff and members of the public from potential harm such as injury, loss and emotional distress. Sophisticated analyses and decision-making are required to properly balance the rights of the public and service workers to be free from harm with those of individual service users, and to meet the current demand for greater public accountability and transparency in the decision-making process.

Many of the issues we face today are immediate and practical rather than abstract or theoretical and based in the reality of providing community services rather than aspiration. Experience over the last twenty years has revealed how, given the opportunity, some people with intellectual disabilities will flourish in community settings and grow. For others, living in the community has been an altogether more challenging experience. The precision and robustness of the supports necessary for people who find community living challenging have sometimes been lacking. Behaviours that pose little or no apparent risk in segregated settings are apt to be viewed differently in integrated community settings. Poorly matched support leads inevitably to more challenging behaviour, which is known to be associated with increased risks of injury, loss, abuse, neglect, exclusion, rejection, social isolation and impaired development, together with dysfunctional stress among staff.

The ambitious nature of the task started some twenty years ago continues to exert influence over the nature of risks we face today and the degree of exposure to those risks. This applies as much to global decisions about investing in more or less restrictive service models for people whose support needs are challenging as to individual assessments of specific actions as they relate to a particular person within a given situation at a given point in time. High expectations create new demands. New demands generate ambitious goals. Ambitious goals require innovation and development. Innovation and development carry risk. In all cases the potential risks associated with a particular action need to be identified, assessed and managed in relation to the potential benefits of that action. The fundamental questions are always the same. What are the potential benefits and harms, who might they affect, and how likely are they to occur? How do we maximise the potential benefits and minimise the potential harms?

Prepared for BILD by Sharon Powell, this good practice guide sets out in clear and simple terms a structured and systematic approach to the identification, assessment and management of risks associated with challenging behaviours.

The guide covers philosophical and organisational issues and the nature of risk and risk-taking before going on to describe good practice in working with risk. Checklists and pro formas are provided to aid working with and assessing risk in such a way that nothing is overlooked or accidentally omitted and every stage is transparent and clear. There is a section covering common problems in risk assessment where things might go wrong as a result of frame blindness, overconfidence or over-investment in expert solutions. Physical interventions are specifically discussed in the context of risk assessment.

Applying the procedural guidance this guide provides should enable us to improve the lives of people with intellectual and developmental disabilities by improving the identification of issues where formal risk assessment is necessary, improving the quality of our decisions about risk and risk management, increasing our confidence in the decisions we make, and providing the means of demonstrating publicly the quality, content and process of the decision we make.

Dr Sandy Toogood BCBA

Introduction

Risk is an evolving concept; it is changing and rarely stays the same from one day to the next. As individuals we are prepared to take calculated risks in our daily lives for a variety of reasons. As professionals we are expected to identify and manage risk in an objective manner.

Reactive strategies for the management of risk when behaviour challenges should form part of an overall framework. This should include approaches that support positive behaviour. Physical interventions must be used only as a last resort.

This guide has been designed to help with establishing a framework to support individuals with learning disabilities or autistic spectrum disorders whose behaviour challenges services and presents a risk to themselves or others.

Philosophical and organisational issues

Organisational foundations

Organisations have a responsibility to ensure that where service users' behaviour presents significant risks to themselves or others a framework exists that will enable staff to respond appropriately.

The organisational framework for working with risk should include clear policies on key issues, together with agreed procedures for implementing those policies in practice.

Policies

- ethical working practices
- protection of vulnerable people from abuse
- risk management
- health and safety
- prevention and management of challenging behaviour
- use of physical interventions

Procedures

- strategy for dissemination of organisational policies
- person centred planning, including lifestyle planning
- implementation of individualised support plans
- training strategy

The nature of risk

Risk may be categorised in a number of ways.

Risk of harm to self

- intentionally, for example self-injurious behaviour
- unintentionally, through neglect of self

Risk of harm to others

- as a result of behaviours exhibited
- to relatives, friends, fellow service users, staff and the public

Risk of harm from others

- emotional abuse
- physical abuse
- sexual abuse
- financial abuse
- from relatives, friends, fellow service users, staff and the public

Significant risk of harm to property

- may increase risk to self, for example punching glass
- may increase risk to others, for example throwing heavy objects
- may damage or destroy scarce resources, for example specialist equipment

Taking risks

We all face risks, great and small, in every aspect of our lives. Those we decide to take, we try to rationalise.

Figure 1: Taking risks

Risk	Rationale
Daily:	
Using our car	Benefits outweigh the risk
Smoking	It will not kill me
Drinking alcohol	As long as I drink plenty of water it will not hurt me
Occasional:	
Flying	Benefits outweigh the risk
Taking a foreign holiday	Individual risk is low
Talking to a stranger	Better than being alone
Dream risks:	
Bungee jumping	Wanting to do something dangerous so badly that the risks seem irrelevant
Extreme sports	
Deep sea diving	

As you can see from the table, we may take frequent risks based on a very flimsy rationale. There is frequently little reasoned thinking behind the way most of us weigh up risk in our own lives. We tend to take risks on a day-to-day basis without much consideration for the process of assessment and decision-making. Interestingly, we are also prepared to take the occasional large risk in the name of our dream – the 'what makes life worth living' factor. This is acceptable when it is ourselves we are placing at risk in our private lives. It is not when in our professional work we are assessing risk to others.

Procedures for working with risk

Using less subjective and more objective and professional ways of calculating risk for others requires taking a broad and holistic view of the circumstances and individuals concerned. One way of achieving this is to develop and use checklists in key areas to ensure that all major issues are taken into account. A number of checklists are provided as part of this guide. The use of three of them is explained below, and the remaining four are covered in the later section *The risk assessment process*.

Developing risk policies

We have already examined the organisational foundations of working with risk in challenging behaviour. Calculating risk must always be considered together with issues of policy as part of the organisational framework for working with challenging behaviour. Risk assessment should never be implemented in isolation from a clear service policy and a developed common approach within that service towards risk assessment. Both need to relate to the support of individual service users on a person-centred basis. They may be evolved using the *Checklist for developing risk policies* included in this guide.

Service user vulnerability

Aspects of a person or a lifestyle may increase the likelihood of behaviour which challenges. In individual service users these must be identified as a basis for risk assessment. Some key factors of this kind can be found in the *Checklist for service user vulnerability*. A *Pro forma for assessment of service user vulnerability* is also provided in this resource.

Breaking confidentiality

Confidentiality is a fundamental aspect of ethical approaches to working with people who present challenging behaviour. But a conflict of interest may occur where an individual is assessed as presenting a significant risk due to identified behaviours, and this risk is posed in more than one service used by that individual. There may be a clear need for one service to share information with others in the best interests of the service user, or in the public interest.

In many circumstances, with a full explanation, service users will be happy to give consent to confidentiality being broken. The service providing the information is responsible for ensuring that this consent is informed and valid.

Even so, careful consideration must be given before sharing any information which has been gained in confidence. A service has to act appropriately and reasonably, with due regard for the human rights of the individual concerned. The facts shared must be relevant to a specific risk, and not irrelevant personal information.

Factors which indicate that sharing of information is essential can be found in the *Checklist for breaking confidentiality* included in this guide.

Why assess risk?

We have earlier examined the often flimsy basis on which we assess and rationalise the risks we decide to take in our private lives. In our professional roles we are rightly expected to be more objective and evidence-based about risk. We seek to support people appropriately to get the most out of their lives while also being clear about the dangers they may run and doing our best to manage these. Being subjective can cause problems with this, usually in terms of two extremes.

One problem is that, as individuals, all of us are prepared to take a variety of calculated risks in life and this may translate into our professional practice. Often the type of risk we are prepared to take personally will be reflected in our opinion of what may or may not be a reasonable risk for someone we are supporting. This may reduce the quality of our judgement in risk assessment and lead to inappropriate risk management and the exposure of service users to unjustifiable hazards.

The other extreme is that we translate our own fears and concerns, become over-protective and do not allow for an acceptable element of risk. This can remove some of the joy of life – the anticipation and excitement we all get from the unpredictable elements of living. People have a right not to be wrapped in cotton wool or cocooned. They must be allowed take reasonable risks in pursuit of their dreams.

The elements of risk

For the above reasons we must be objective in calculating risk. To begin with, this means identifying the elements of the risk and taking account of all variables that may affect the degree of risk from a target behaviour. An initial assessment of an individual should leave us aware of the factors present that will affect the immediate risk.

Figure 2: Risk factors

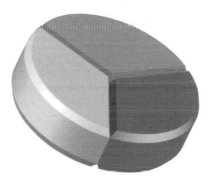

The individual:
personality, history, behaviours which challenge, known triggers

The environment:
temperature, light, other people and noise, as they affect the individual's behaviour

The potential outcomes:
possible positive and negative results of the individual's behaviour

Assessing risk

Risk scoring

There may sometimes be confusion between factors such as the frequency of a risk or its duration (Fig. 3) and the actual degree of risk (Fig. 4). The following risk score chart is designed to identify how high a risk is regardless of these factors.

Figure 3: Frequency of risk

Behaviour/ consequence	Base score	Less than 4 times a month	4 to 8 times a month	Up to 15 times a month	At least once daily
1. Severe injury to self or others which requires immediate emergency medical attention	4	8	12	16	20
2. Injury to self or others that requires non urgent medical attention	3	6	9	12	15
3. Behaviour which may result in a criminal offence being committed	4	8	12	16	20
4. Minor injury to self or others	2	4	6	8	10
5. No Injury to any individual although significant damage to property occurs	1	2	3	4	5

Figure 4: Degree of risk

Score	Rating of risk	Action status
1–3	Low	Identify target behaviours in behaviour support plan, monitor and review monthly
4–7	Medium	Develop and implement a risk assessment, monitor weekly and review monthly
8–15	High	Prioritise behaviour management plan and risk assessment issues, monitor closely and review weekly
16–20	Critical	Requires immediate action, daily monitoring and review of the risks presented

Example

Behaviour/consequence: Fred hits out at staff and other householders when he doesn't understand the social situation he is in or is having difficulty in communicating with other people. Frequently this results in injury to others, such as small abrasions and grazes. (behaviour 2 = base score 3)

Frequency: This has occurred 5 times in the past month. (score 9)

Behaviour/consequence	= base score 3
Frequency	= score 9
Total	**= score 12**

A total score of 12 indicates that this behaviour has a high degree of risk and requires immediate and continuing action.

Identifying hazards and risks

This can seem complicated. But the basics are straightforward.

Figure 5: Health & Safety Executive definitions (1999)

hazard	**risk**
anything that could cause harm	the chance, high or low, that somebody will be harmed by the hazard

The Health & Safety Executive are experts in this field. Their guide (1999) on how to assess risks in the workplace is relevant to any environment in which dangers might arise. It is broken down into clear stages:

1. Look for the hazards.

2. Decide who might be harmed and how.

3. Evaluate the risks and decide whether the existing precautions are adequate or whether more should be done.

4. Record your findings.

5. Review your assessment and revise it if necessary.

The risk assessment process

Once information has been gathered on hazards and risks, the most important element is the articulation of identified risk. Articulation is essentially the statement of the risk in such a way that it is easily identified and understood. A fuller explanation is given a little later in this guide.

Clear plain language should always be used in the context of risk assessment. This simplifies planning and improves quality in risk management.

Like identification of hazards and risks the following process of assessing and managing risk can also be broken down into stages:

1. information gathering

2. planning and consultation

3. implementation and monitoring

4. evaluation and review

As with procedures for working with risk generally, checklists can be used to ensure that risk assessment is carried out comprehensively. A checklist for each of the above four stages is included in this guide.

Describing the challenging behaviour

Think about the behaviour:

- What do you and other people supporting the individual know about the history and background to the target behaviour?

- Do you know when it started?

- What was happening in the person's life when it started to become challenging and to affect the person's life?

- Is it a new behaviour or has it happened for some time?

- Is it similar to other behaviours that have been a challenge in the past?

- What does the person do when not exhibiting the identified challenging behaviour?

Articulating risk

This means clearly distinguishing and describing the parts or elements of a risk.

The process of articulating risk is important in setting up the appropriate strategies to deal with the risk in terms that can be clearly understood. This enables the behaviour to be recognised and the relevant response to be implemented by all the people supporting the individual.

Articulation of risk can be broken down into five components:

1. **The behaviour**
    This should be described so that anyone can recognise the behaviour and know that this is the point at which to begin putting into effect the appropriate behavioural support plan and the strategies for reducing the impact of that behaviour.

2. **Element of risk**
    This is the degree of risk that is presented by the target behaviour. Who is most at risk – the individual, or others who may be affected as a consequence of the behaviour?

3. **Primary strategies**

    These are strategies which are part of a behaviour support plan. They enable the person to avoid socially less valid challenging behaviours by encouraging them to be involved in more worthwhile daily activities. Some may also be used as a precaution in the event of the individual exhibiting key signs that the identified behaviour may occur.

4. **Secondary strategies**

    These are distraction or defusion strategies for de-escalating a situation. They may assist in avoiding or reducing the behaviour identified as a risk.

5. **Reactive strategies**

    These are strategies designed to be used in the short term. They are usually behaviour management techniques or physical interventions that enable carers to keep the individual and others safe while at the same time implementing longer term behaviour change strategies.

Managed and unmanaged risk

Managed risk:

-   has been subject to full risk assessment procedures

-   has a written risk assessment and a full behavioural plan

-   includes behaviour change strategies in its management planning

-   does not see reactive interventions as a long-term solution

-   aims to manage a person's challenging behaviours or the risk posed by those behaviours

Behaviour change strategies will be required to help achieve short-term control over challenging behaviour and to develop adaptive, functionally equivalent or functionally alternative behaviours in the medium and long term.
Allen (2001)

Unmanaged risk:

-   must be disclosed to all involved if it presents a significant hazard to the service user or others

-   must be clearly identified in planning in accordance with the advice in this resource

-   must be subject to appropriate health and safety procedures in line with organisational and legal requirements

The assessment process

A basic component of any risk assessment of challenging behaviour is the assessment process itself. Team discussions can support this. Important questions to ask yourself and your colleagues include:

- How well do we really know this person? Do we understand what motivates the individual?

  What does the behaviour mean to the person? Why might someone indulge in such behaviours? Often this can be difficult for us to empathise with, particularly when the behaviour is harmful to the person or other people.

- What is being communicated? Is it being received and understood?

- Why is this behaviour regarded as challenging? Is it a problem for the individual, for others or for the organisation supporting them?

  What causes the behaviour to emerge? For example, a behaviour may gain a needed service, object or attention. What else makes that behaviour worthwhile to the person or encourages it to occur?

- What is the degree of challenge? For example, is the behaviour life-threatening? Or is it just disruptive?

- Is the behaviour worsening or likely to become worse?

- Are other behaviours likely to improve if the targeted behaviour does?

- Does the behaviour interfere with opportunities for the person to experience life opportunities? Will quality of life improve for the individual if the behaviour is better managed?

This process should be supported by use of the *Checklist for information gathering*, the *Pro forma for behaviour description*, and the *Pro forma for articulating risk*.

What might go wrong?

Mistakes can be made. It is important when reviewing the process to actively look for and take account of possible difficulties that can arise from flawed approaches to risk assessment.

Common problems to look for include the following:

1. **Frame blindness**

    This is where a group of professionals solve the wrong problem. One cause is that inaccurate information has been recorded, leading the team to deal with an issue not relevant to the target behaviour. Another is making assumptions on insufficient evidence.

2. **Overconfidence**

    This can arise from too much confidence in the team decision-making process. It may lead to risk assessment being based on insufficient or inaccurate information, or purely on the views of people directly involved in supporting the individual.

3. **Failure to monitor and review**

    This often happens due to poor time management. Too much of the available time has been invested in the assessment process, leaving not enough for monitoring and review, which is then left to chance. This can lead to missed opportunities in reassessing the level of risk and re-evaluating the most appropriate response to a target behaviour.

4. **The 'expert' myth**

    The is the idea that a team of 'experts' will always get it right. This leads to group failure to assess and question the whole picture. It may result in attempts to implement an inappropriate support plan based on a faulty risk assessment.

5. **Rushing**

    This is not assessing the situation fully, plunging in and so missing important information. It can result in risk assessments which fail to identify hazards and the dangers they pose.

6. **Failure to audit**

    This is failing to obtain and use accurate and up-to-date records to audit the risk assessment and behavioural plan. It may be linked to earlier mistakes in monitoring and review and can leave individuals, both service users and providers, exposed to unmanaged risk.

Physical interventions in the context of risk assessment

All people with a learning disability or autistic spectrum disorder who may exhibit challenging behaviour have a right to appropriate behaviour management plans as part of their risk assessment. These should include a range of positive strategies developing on a three-part gradient.

The third level will include reactive strategies involving physical interventions where the target behaviour has been assessed as presenting a sufficiently significant risk. However, this should be seen in the context of strategies at the two previous levels designed in part to avoid the need for physical intervention.

Level 1: Proactive primary strategies

These include enabling the individual to develop socially acceptable behaviours to achieve objectives which act as alternatives to challenging behaviour. To be effective, such strategies need to be maintained over a long period of time.

Level 2: Secondary prevention strategies

These strategies, for example defusion and distraction, enable carers to manage and de-escalate a target behaviour in an appropriate and individualised way.

Level 3: Reactive strategies

These could include breakaway techniques and the use of restrictive physical interventions.

It is important that reactive strategies are not used as methods of managing behaviour where there are more appropriate methods of supporting the individual, such as those identified for levels 1 and 2. Ideally they should be used only in the short term while more acceptable approaches are developed through the risk assessment and behavioural plan process. There may be cases where such strategies require to be maintained long term, but these should be selected with care and subject to regular review.

Checklists

Procedures for working with risk

Checklist for developing risk policies

Service goals

- What is the service trying to achieve, both long term and short term, via risk management procedures?

Service identity

- What is distinctive about the service?
- Does it specialise in supporting people with specific needs?
- What is the service skill mix?
- Are any legal factors relevant, for example under the Mental Health Act 1983?

Service limits

- What are currently accepted standards of service provision?
- Are there identified service deficiencies?
- Are there known limitations on service provision such as staff shortages?

Service philosophy

- How is the values base of the organisation expressed?
- Is there a mission statement?
- What approaches are there to supporting choice, control, autonomy and self-expression among service users?
- Are services inclusive?

Working with wider policy

- Does the risk policy take account of other relevant organisational policies, procedures or protocols?
- Does it cross-reference with wider policy relating to management of challenging behaviour, adult protection or risk assessment?

Protocols for practice

- Is written clarification provided of statements in the risk policy relating to interventions such as seclusion, time out or chemical restraint in order to guide practice?

Legal and ethical guidelines

- Is there a statement which outlines how the risk management process of the organisation sits within the legal framework?
- Is there a statement of ethical and moral issues relating to the use of physical and other interventions?

Checklist for service user vulnerability

Personality

Some people are more likely to behave in ways which could be described as risky due to their personality type. For example, there are those who are more likely to take part in extreme sports or to lose control of their emotions easily.

History

If a behaviour has led to the emergence of risk in the past this indicates an increased likelihood that the behaviour will present similar problems in the future.

Mental state

In some individuals their mental health may affect the way that they behave and increase the risks they present to themselves, others or their immediate environment.

Unresolved loss or bereavement

Many people with learning disabilities encounter major losses in life which are never acknowledged. For some this can lead to an increase in anxiety levels at times of stress and a consequent increase in challenging behaviour.

Family support systems

Where people have positive relationships with family members this is likely to increase a sense of self-esteem and personal identity and reduce the need to behave in a socially invalid way. On the other hand, separation from family members may have adverse effects on behaviour.

Personal relationships

Sometimes the friendships or associations formed by individuals increase the chances of a challenging behaviour being exhibited. This may be because the person does not like certain people, either staff or other service users.

Occasionally the development of a strong bond between two people who have similar interests or personality traits can increase the chances of challenging behaviour and the risks associated with it.

Environmental factors

Unsuitable surroundings can trigger behaviour that may increase a person's vulnerability to risk. For example, if the environment is highly stimulating this may cause an individual to become aroused and behave in a socially unacceptable manner.

Poor communication skills

Impaired ability in self-expression and communication with others can be extremely frustrating and may increase an individual's predisposition to challenging behaviour.

Frequent moves

Moves are often linked to major bereavements such as loss of friends and familiar surroundings.

Service users may lack understanding as to why these moves have occurred.

It can also be difficult for some people with learning disabilities to adapt to new environments.

Physical illness

When an individual is unwell or is experiencing physical difficulties, this may lead to emergent behaviours that increase vulnerability to risk.

Boredom and isolation

Boredom can affect the way people relate both to others and their environment.

Exhibiting behaviour which could be described as challenging may be more interesting than the alternatives. It may also serve as a way to obtain interaction with other people.

This checklist should be used together with the *Pro forma for assessment of service user vulnerability* provided in this guide.

Checklist for breaking confidentiality

- Where there is risk of harm to members of the public, particularly with vulnerable groups such as children or older people.

- Where the assessed risk may be linked to previous or potential criminal offences.

- Where there is a risk of significant self-harm.

- When the person moves between services, particularly in relation to the individual's support plan.

Risk assessment process

Checklist for information gathering

- Are there hard data? This is specific information, for example records of observable behaviours from ABC charts. This information is not subjective.

- Are there soft data? This is often anecdotal information, perhaps perceptions of behaviours from staff, relatives and the service user. Although this information is frequently subjective, and for that reason must be analysed carefully, it may add a dimension to the data collected that would otherwise be missed.

- Have all information sources available been accessed? This can often be detailed and time-consuming work, but in terms of ensuring the accuracy of the risk assessment it is an important element of the process.

- What are the present risks indicated by the behaviours? Identify and record all risks from behaviours that have been indicated in collected data.

- Historically, has the person behaved in a manner that has presented significant risk?

- Has this risk changed and, if so, how?

- What situational or environmental factors affect the degree of risk and how might these be managed?

Checklist for planning and consultation

- Draft a risk assessment and proposals for managing identified risk for the person concerned.

- At the same time develop a proposed individual positive behaviour management strategy or behavioural support plan.

- Consult on these proposals with all relevant parties. This should include the service user, family members, carers, advocates and other professionals and agencies.

- Where necessary, redraft plans on the basis of feedback from consultations.

- Plan to implement the risk assessment and behavioural support plan in practice. This will include setting out appropriate strategies for responding to specific target behaviours. Where a behaviour occurs in more than one environment it may be appropriate to have a range of differing responses to it.

- Ensure all parties involved have copies of the final plans.

Checklist for implementation and monitoring

- Is everyone involved in supporting the person aware of the risk assessment and behavioural support plan?

- Do all concerned know when and how implementation will begin?

- Is everyone clear on positive approaches to avoiding challenging behaviour, as well as reactive strategies?

- Are the arrangements for monitoring and recording in place before implementation begins? See the following checklist for these.

Checklist for evaluation and review

- Monitor the implementation by keeping accurate records of when the target behaviours have occurred, when a strategy has been implemented, and what reactive strategies have been used.

- Nil returns can also be significant. If an agreed strategy or response has not been implemented in circumstances which called for it, what were the reasons?

- Make sure outcomes are also recorded. Where they have been used, it is important to record key points from debriefings of the service user and others involved in any incident.

- Review the process on a regular basis. It is important that review dates are established at the outset, and kept to as a minimum.

- Evaluate the effectiveness of the implemented plan, and the benefits or otherwise for the service user and others.

- Identify any further assessment or planning required.

- Pick up any change in the level of risk at the earliest possible opportunity. If necessary bring review dates forward and make them more frequent, and consider the need for reassessment.

- At all stages in evaluation and review, look for risks which are unmanaged, the reasons for this, and any steps which may reduce overall risk.

Pro formas

Pro forma for behaviour description

Describe the behaviour observed. For example: 'Threw chair at the window', or 'Banged head on the bed head repeatedly.'	
<ul><li>When does the behaviour occur?</li><li>In which environments does it occur?</li><li>Who is present?</li><li>What else happened that may be significant?</li></ul>	
<ul><li>What may make this behaviour worthwhile to the person?</li><li>What are the immediate consequences of the behaviour for other people?</li><li>What are the immediate consequences of the behaviour for the individual?</li><li>What happens when the behaviour stops?</li><li>Does the person communicate any information which may be helpful?</li></ul>	

Pro forma for articulating risk

Identified or target behaviour	Environment in which the behaviour occurs	Element of risk and risk factors	Primary preventative strategies	Secondary preventative strategies	Reactive strategies

Pro forma for assessment of service user vulnerability

History – What are the previous behaviours that have had an impact on the individual's life?	
Mental state – Does the person's psychological standing affect behaviours significantly?	
Loss issues – Has the person suffered a recent loss or have unresolved grief issues?	
Family support – Does the person have support networks?	
Friendships – Are there significant relationships in the persons life?	
Environmental issues – Are there any significant environmental issues which may trigger challenging behaviour?	
Communication – What form of self-expression does the individual prefer to use?	
Personal factors – Has the person experienced frequent moves, abuse or are other issues relevant?	
Drugs and alcohol – Does the person have any history of using drugs, prescribed or other or alcohol?	
Physical illness – Might the individual have health problems which affect engagement with others or the environment?	
Daily activities – Is the person occupied, with a fulfilling life, opportunities to enjoy favourite activities and an active social life?	

References

Allen, D (2001) *Training Carers in Physical Interventions: Research Towards Evidence Based Practice* Kidderminster, BILD

Health & Safety Executive (1999) *Five steps to risk assessment* Sudbury, HSE